HOW TO SPEAK
CAT!

A Marshall Edition
Conceived, edited, and designed by Marshall Editions
The Old Brewery
6 Blundell Street
London N7 9BH

ISBN-13: 978-0-545-02079-4
ISBN-10: 0-545-02079-4

Publisher: Richard Green
Commissioning editor: Claudia Martin
Art director: Ivo Marloh
Managing editor: Paul Docherty
Senior designer: Sarah Robson
Project editor: Amy Head
Design: Alec Chin
Layout: Angela English
Cover photography: John Daniels
Indexer: Lynn Bresler
Production: Nikki Ingram

Printed and bound in China by 1010 Printing International Ltd

08 09 10 11 12 10 9 8 7 6 5 4 3 2 1

First printing, October 2008

HOW TO SPEAK CAT!

By Sarah Whitehead

SCHOLASTIC

Contents

Introduction

Cats are part of our social history. In days gone by, we relied on them to hunt mice and rats and to protect our stores of food. Now we love them for the affection and fun that they bring. However, cats have not lost their "wild side." This is what makes them such fascinating creatures: They are both wild animals and gentle pets!

Our cats are expressive, playful, loving, and fun. They are also independent, cool, determined, and focused. As owners, our job is to try to understand and appreciate both sides of our cats' personalities and to take the time to learn their language so that we can recognize their moods, needs, and feelings.

Although cats have lived side by side with people throughout the centuries and have made their homes on our sofas, it's important to understand that we have to teach each individual cat how to cope with our domestic lives. Cats need to learn to accept all kinds of sights, sounds, and smells in their everyday lives with us, as well as learn to enjoy being touched and handled. They need to be able to cope with the sound of the washing machine, the roar of the vacuum cleaner, the toaster popping up, and our rushing about! They need to be able to ignore the telephone ringing, tolerate being handled at the vet's, and fit in with all the other weird and wonderful experiences that are part of life with humans!

Life with humans must seem strange from a cat's point of view!

Cats "talk" with their bodies and facial expressions.

Most important of all, however, cats need to learn how to communicate with people. It's up to us to teach them a little about human language, while we learn a little "feline." Cats can communicate in ways that humans can barely understand. Their sense of smell is so highly developed that they sometimes "taste" odors rather than just smell them. Their hearing is so acute that they can detect the rustle of a mouse or an insect, and they can see things that we could never spot. Despite all these differences, it is possible to communicate with your cat. By learning how she "talks," you can start to understand her needs and feelings. You will do this by watching her body language and facial expressions. Cats may not speak English, but they can tell us a lot by the movements of their ears, tails, and whiskers!

Learning to understand your cat is fun and interesting and will allow you to interact with her in a way that makes her feel comfortable and secure. You will be able to train her to come when you call, sit and stay, and even do a few tricks for fun!

Very few people take the time to learn how to speak cat. If you do, you will join a lucky group of people who have discovered its rewards. Learning to interpret your cat's behavior will make you an expert on understanding your best friend. She will love you for it!

The feline equivalent of shaking hands? Rubbing is an important part of cat communication.

You and Your Cat

Cats are a joy to live with! They can become great friends, playing with you when they feel active and snuggling on your knee when they simply want affection. Just like us, all cats are different. Some are extroverted and bouncy, others are quiet and shy. Finding out your cat's individual likes and dislikes can be fun.

Caring for your best friend means taking her needs into account when considering her health, behavior, and comfort. All cats need food, water, and several comfortable places to rest! They need to be able to express natural behaviors in order to stay fit and healthy in mind and body.

They also need security, companionship, and exercise to keep them happy. However, your duties and responsibilities as an ideal owner go far beyond basic needs! Cats love to be included as a part of the family. Your cat can enjoy interacting with you, your friends, and even other pets. It is up to us to make sure they fit in right from the start.

Playing with your kitten will help build a bond for life.

A lifelong companion—the responsibilities and joys of cat ownership

Owning a cat is a big responsibility. Although they are known for their independence, cats need us to keep them safe and provide for them so that they have a fulfilled and contented life. Cats give back just as much. They are wonderful companions, enjoying close physical contact and affection just as much as games and fun!

Enjoying quiet time with your kitten is as important as play.

Kittenhood

When we think of kittens we all think of fluffy, cute balls of fun, rolling and playing with their littermates. Kittens are like little sponges, soaking up everything about the world that they have been born into. The fact that cats have had an association with humans for many centuries does not make them instant pets, however. Each and every kitten needs to become used to the sounds, sights, and smells of humans in order to feel comfortable with us. Indeed, feral kittens (cats that are born without homes or owners) miss out on this kind of contact. As a result they are wild, though some eventually learn to tolerate human company. Being handled and becoming familiar with lots of different people is essential for our pets so that they truly enjoy being with us.

Adolescence

Cats have a teenage stage just like humans do. They usually reach their adult size by six to eight months, but continue to mature until they are about two years old. Adolescent cats can look at bit gangly while they grow into their legs and skin! During this stage it's important that you stand by your house rules with your cat. Try some training with her, just for fun. Keep her active

Once adult, cats learn to fit in with our routines.

Old age

Cats tend to age very gracefully. They don't seem to suffer from the same stiffness and lack of energy that old dogs (and humans!) seem to. Even though elderly cats may sleep more, they still enjoy activities indoors or excursions outside, and some still manage to catch rodents or moths! However, more than anything older cats seem to appreciate the love and company of their human caretakers and enjoy being at the heart of their family.

Your cat's real age

The lifespan of a healthy cat is 14–15 years or even longer. This means that your cat can be regarded as a teenager when she's only five months old, an adult at a year old, and a retiree when she's 12! To find an accurate calculation of your cat's "real" age, based on breed, type, and health, visit one of the dedicated Web sites listed on page 92.

and amused with lots of games and puzzles to prevent her natural curiosity from getting her into mischief!

Adult years

Adult cats should look lithe, sleek, athletic, and muscular. If allowed outdoors they can develop a territory that is a mile or more in circumference. They will patrol this territory and use their sense of smell to find out which other cats have been in the area. Adult cats will have learned about your routines and lifestyle. Don't be surprised if yours is waiting on the doorstep when you come home from school or sitting beside her food bowl at exactly the right time for dinner—all this without a wristwatch!

Eight-week-old kitten

Adult cat

Elderly cat

The first days

Your kitten's first days and weeks have a long-term impact on her future life and behavior. Most kittens stay with their mom until they are seven weeks old. This is a very important stage in their lives as they learn how to be a cat and find out about the world around them.

Kittens are born blind and deaf and are completely dependent on their mother for food, warmth, and care. She even helps them go to the toilet. However, they already have a powerful sense of smell. You can see how important this is from the sheer size of a newborn kitten's nose! Even newborn kittens can identify the smell of their mother. They wriggle their way towards her to feed, following her comforting smell.

Purring approval

Kittens are able to purr right from birth. This acts as essential communication between the kittens and their mother to let her know that they are feeding and content. As you know, cats continue to purr throughout their lives to show contentment.

Bright-eyed and inquisitive, kittens need to learn how to be cats from their mom and littermates.

The bond between mother and kittens is forged by scent and sound.

From milk to solid food

When kittens are about four weeks old, their mother starts to wean them off milk and on to solid food. She does this by denying them access to her teats, because their sharp little teeth begin to hurt! Although the kittens will try to get milk from her for a while, they will soon start to look for other food instead, and in this way they begin to use their hunting instincts. They also spend long hours playing hunting games with one another, in which they pounce, chase, attack, and defend—all in a pretend battle!

Litter-training

Cats have an excellent sense of smell and like to wash themselves. This means that cats are usually easy to house-train, but it also means that their litter box needs to be kept in pristine condition. Some cats will avoid using the litter box if it is not kept very clean. Always wash your hands after cleaning the litter box.

The perfect bathroom!

Cats like privacy when they go to the toilet, so their litter box needs to be placed somewhere quiet and out of the way of other pets in the household. Some litter boxes are designed with a roof, walls, and a cat flap for a door. These have the advantage of keeping nosy dogs out! The type of litter you choose should be fine and able to be raked—such as sand or fuller's earth (absorbent particles of dried clay). Litter particles with deodorants in them might make a cat's litter box more pleasant for us, but they probably smell far too strong to most cats!

Most kittens will already be litter-trained when you bring them home, as this is such a natural instinct. If your kitty seems reluctant to use the box, gently place her on it every hour, then praise her and give her a reward if she uses it. Never punish your cat if she goes to the toilet in the wrong place. This might be a sign of anxiety and getting angry at her will only make it worse.

Hiding and pouncing games are always favorites!

TOP TIP

Do you have more than one cat? Then you need more than one litter box! You need one box for each cat, plus one extra, to be safe.

Home sweet home

Having a new kitten can be great fun, but like all young animals, they need to learn a routine and some house rules. Sit down with your family and decide on which rules you think are important, right from the outset. Decide who is responsible for feeding and find an appropriate "dining" place.

Cat naps

Your kitten should have a bed of her own in a place that is quiet and undisturbed. Many cats love hammocks, while others like enclosed, "igloo style" beds where they can feel cozy and secure. Although cats are experts at finding the perfect place to sleep, it may be a good idea to prevent your kitten from sleeping on your bed or on top of the computer if you don't want her to do this later on in life. Make a list of the places your cat is allowed to sleep and those that are out of bounds. That way, no one will have an excuse to break the rules!

Picking your kitten up safely

Make sure that you support your kitten's body weight in your hands when you pick her up. Your kitten needs to be held closely, but not too tightly, in order to feel secure. Cats that don't enjoy being picked up can be a real problem at the vet's later in life, so it's a good idea to pick your kitten up and place her on a raised surface from time to time, then give her a tasty treat. This will mean that she has pleasant associations with being picked up.

Feeding frenzy

Make sure your kitten has her own feeding dishes and water bowl. Never feed her from your own plate or give her tidbits from the table. This will only encourage her to jump up and steal food from the kitchen counter or get onto the dining room table in the hope of finding something delicious to eat! Some cats might even start to steal food right out of your hands while you are eating—very rude! Decide whether you are going to feed your cat at set mealtimes, or whenever she asks for food.

The best table

Cats like to eat in a place where they feel safe. It is sensible to choose one area and use it consistently so your cat learns that she will be fed there each time. Feeding her on a raised surface will make her feel safe. She will be able to look around while she eats and will also be out of the way of feet walking past and the intrusion of other pets. Make sure you feed your cat well away from her litter tray. Neither animals nor humans like eating in their bathrooms, after all!

Cats are naturally clean creatures—they rake up the litter to cover traces of where they have been.

Your kitten's litter box should be placed well away from her food and water bowls and her bed.

CAT FACT

Cats cannot be vegetarian. This is because their bodies are unable to manufacture an essential amino acid called taurine, which is vital for their eyes to function properly. They need to get their taurine from meat instead. Always feed a good quality cat food, as recommended by your vet.

Warm supper

Cats tend to enjoy their food much more when it's at room temperature, because the smell and taste of food is stronger when it is warm. For this reason it's best to take her food out of the fridge for a short time, perhaps half an hour, before you feed it to her.

Dining companions

Unlike dogs, most cats are very happy to have company while they eat. Talking to your cat quietly and stroking her gently while she is eating can help to build a bond between you. This is a good way for anxious cats to learn to associate human contact with something positive! If your cat is especially nervous, it might even be a good idea to split up her food into tiny portions. This way you can feed her small amounts often throughout the day and use every opportunity to have calm, friendly interactions with her.

The great outdoors

The decision of whether to let your cat have free access to the outdoors can be difficult. If you live near a busy road or you are concerned that your cat could be hurt or lost, then keeping her indoors might be best.

However, cats are active predators! Just like their wild lion and tiger cousins, they love to hunt and roam. This gives them exercise and mental stimulation, as well as fun. If you decide to keep your cat indoors permanently, then it's essential that you give her lots of activities to keep her occupied.

Cats are in their element outdoors, where they can run and jump.

Important protection

Kittens need to have completed their vaccinations before they are allowed out into the big, wide world. The appropriate time can vary, so ask your vet when you can let her out. Even if your kitten has completed her vaccinations when you bring her home, or you have an older cat, she will still need to be kept indoors for three to four weeks before being allowed out. This is to allow her to become familiar with your house and attached to you, so that when you do let her out, she will want to come home again!

CAT FACT
Cats have an excellent homing instinct. This means that they are usually very good at finding their way back home using sight and scent. Some cats have even been known to track their route home from hundreds of miles away!

TOP TIP

Make sure you always fit a collar that has a breakaway mechanism, that way the collar will come off if she gets caught on something.

Not safe to allow your cat out on her own? Train her to walk on a leash instead.

Collar care

Your kitten will need to wear a collar if she's going to venture outdoors once her vaccinations are complete. This takes some getting used to! Start with a tiny, lightweight kitten collar. Put it on while your kitten is eating to begin with, then remove it again. Repeat this often. It will help her associate the collar

with good things. Make sure you can fit a finger under the collar so that it's not too tight, and keep checking the fit as she grows.

Let me out!

Follow the suggestions below to make sure your cat comes home safely the first time you allow her out.

1 Let your kitten or cat out early in the day. This gives her time to explore, but still come home before it gets dark.

2 Make sure you have some delicious, smelly food, such as fish, prepared for your cat before you let her out. You can then give her some of this food as a reward as soon as she comes home.

3 Cats have scent glands between the pads of their paws. This means it is important to allow your cat to walk out of the door on the first few occasions, rather than lifting her outside. This way she will be able to follow her own scent to get home.

4 Keep other pets indoors the first few times you allow your kitten or cat outside. Dogs can sometimes chase cats when they get excited. This could scare your cat badly and make her fearful about returning home.

Hazards in the home and outdoors

Cats are very curious creatures. They have the agility to squeeze through gaps and climb onto high surfaces. Sometimes this gets them into trouble! Make sure that your home is as safe as you can make it—especially if your cat is a kitten.

Toxic dangers

Unfortunately, kittens are often interested in the insides of garages and garden sheds, where they might come across chemicals and other harmful substances. Car antifreeze is particularly dangerous because it tastes sweet and seems to attract cats. Always take your kitten to the vet if you suspect that she has eaten something that may be a risk to her health.

In the home

Cats love to play with all kinds of things. At the top of their list are things that make rustling sounds and things that look like prey. Unfortunately, this means that items such as foil-wrapped pills are tempting, which can be life threatening to your cat if swallowed. Your kitten may find it fun to play with a length of string, but electric cables, which look similar, are obviously very dangerous. Try to think about how your cat would see things and make sure risky items are safely out of the way.

Plant risks

Cats will often chew on grass when outdoors. This does them no harm. However, eating certain plants can be unsafe. Some of these are kept as houseplants, making them a risk for cats that are kept indoors. Cyclamen, ficus, umbrella plants (schefflera), and poinsettias are all toxic examples.

Climbing practice may be fun, but it may not be safe for kittens or good for curtains.

Kittens seem to be attracted to plants, so make sure they are nontoxic.

Other cats

Cats are very territorial. This means they will defend their garden or an area that they have claimed as their own. Although most cats would rather run than fight, occasionally disputes between neighboring cats do occur, and then fights can break out. If you think your kitten has been involved in a scuffle with another cat, check her over very carefully or take her to the vet for a thorough examination. Cat bites can be difficult to find, but they nearly always result in an abscess or infection, which needs to be treated.

Other animals

In some areas, venomous snakes and other creatures, such as lizards or even eagles, may be a risk to your kitten. Ask your vet for advice on this and take steps to protect your kitten from danger. Kittens are occasionally stung by wasps or bees, usually when they have been chasing them! Although this may be painful for your cat it does not usually cause any problems. It does mean that your cat will be more respectful next time! Occasionally, kittens find frogs or toads in the yard, and they cannot resist trying to play with them. However, some toads have a special

coating on their skin that will irritate the cat's mouth if she tries to bite it, causing the cat to foam around the mouth. This can be quite distressing for your cat and for you! Contact your vet if your pet seems unwell.

QUICK QUIZ

Do you know how to keep your kitten safe? Score one point for each correct answer, then add up your score to see how safe your kitten is!

1. Which of these plants is poisonous to your kitten?
a) Poinsettia
b) Grass
c) Lettuce

2. What should you do if your kitten looks sick?
a) Take her to the vet.
b) Stroke her.
c) Cover her up with a blanket.

3. Your kitten wants to play, so you should
a) Let her choose what she wants to play with.
b) Use a specially designed cat toy.
c) Don't play at all.

4. Your kitten is bored while you watch TV. She tries chewing at an electric cable. You should:
a) Scold her for being naughty.
b) Ignore her. You don't want to miss your favorite program.
c) Get her a safe toy to keep her occupied.

5. You are going to allow your kitten outside for the first time. You should:
a) Put her out at night and hope she comes back.
b) Allow her out first thing in the morning and then call her back in for some food before it's dark.
c) Carry her outside and stay with her.

Answers: 1. (a) 2. (a) 3. (b) 4. (c) 5. (b)

Health and grooming

To keep your kitten in the peak of health, you will need to handle and groom her every day. This should be enjoyable for you both, and will also help you to bond and become the best of friends. At the same time, you can do a quick health check—so play at being the vet and look in her ears, eyes, and at her teeth and claws. You could even get a play stethoscope and listen to her heartbeat!

Handling your cat every day will ensure that she's confident and calm at the vet's.

Home health check

Eyes

Your cat's eyes should be clear and bright, with no discharge or redness. Cats have a third eyelid, which covers the eye if your cat is unwell. If you see this, you should take your kitten to the vet.

Ears

Cats have upright ears, so it is usually easy to see a little way into the ear canal. This should look clean and pink. If there is a brown discharge visible or if there is an unpleasant smell, your cat might have ear mites or an ear infection. Cats with ear problems often shake their heads, too, so this is another symptom to look out for. Never poke anything, such as a cotton swab, into your cat's ear. Instead, take her to the vet if she has an ear problem.

Teeth

Your cat's teeth should look clean and white. It's a good idea to gently touch and open your kitten's mouth while she is a kitten so she gets used to it. You might need to give her special cat pills if she gets sick one day! Ask an adult to help you hold your cat while you look at her teeth, so that she stays calm and does not scratch you.

Essential for longhair cats, grooming should be gentle but thorough.

For longhair cats, finish the grooming session by gently combing through the hair, separating the strands. Do not pull or tug if you find a knot. It is better to tease these apart or even trim them out than to hurt your cat by pulling her hair.

For shorthair cats, "polish" her coat by using a velvet grooming mitt, stroking in the direction of the coat. This makes the coat gleam!

Make your shorthair cat gleam by stroking her with a velvet mitt.

Good grooming

All cats benefit from grooming, but longhair cats need to be brushed and combed much more regularly than shorthair ones.

1 Start by brushing your cat down her back, from head to tail. Most cats enjoy this as long as you are gentle and the brush feels comfortable.

2 Move on to brushing down the shoulders and back legs.

3 Give your cat some treats intermittently to reward good behavior. If she fidgets, it's a good idea to smear a little anchovy paste or another tasty treat onto an upright surface at cat-nose height. Your cat can then be busy licking at the paste while you brush her!

TO SPOT A SICK KITTY

Take your cat to the vet if she shows these signs. Your cat:

- [ ] Is refusing to eat
- [ ] Has an upset tummy or is vomiting
- [ ] Is drinking more than usual
- [ ] Doesn't want to play
- [ ] Is very sleepy all the time
- [ ] Is not grooming herself or you can see the third eyelid across her eye

Learning Cat Language

Cats have their own unique language, but they don't communicate with words or sentences. Instead, cats have a complex system of body signals, facial expressions, and sounds that they make to express how they are feeling. Perhaps even more remarkable is the fact that cats use scent to "talk" to one another. This is a very important part of feline communication, but one that humans are often completely unaware of.

Kittens learn how to use body language from their mother and littermates, figuring out how to communicate with one another and understand the body signals of other cats. They also need to learn about how humans communicate. Cats don't smile, laugh, wave their arms, or shout when they are excited, so they have to learn that these gestures are not a threat. Just like learning any new language, studying "feline" takes time and patience. However, learning about how your best friend communicates will help you interpret exactly what she is saying and reply to her!

Perfect harmony. Two different species, speaking the same language.

Learning "feline" as a second language

Learning "feline" as a second language is a challenge, but is also fun and absorbing. If you are good at watching for tiny hints and clues, you will be an expert in communicating with your cat in no time!

Smelling sense

Cats see the world very differently from us. Their senses are focused on different things, particularly smells. Indeed, scent is probably as important to them as sight is to us! Your cat can glean all kinds of information from scent signals that other cats leave and they can probably tell a lot about us, too! Humans are very poor at recognizing scent in comparison. To us a smell is either nice or nasty. We tend to recognize one another by the way we look and sound, while cats recognize familiar people and other animals by their scents.

If only cats could really talk...

CAT FACT

Each and every kitten needs to learn how to interact with humans, to accept being handled, and to enjoy contact. This must happen between the ages of two and seven weeks old, or the kitten is likely to behave like a wild animal. This means cat breeders must make sure their kittens are handled by lots of different people and that they are used to seeing all the sights and sounds of everyday life in a busy home.

TEST YOURSELF!
How many different types of cat can you name? Try to think about all the different species in the world, from big wildcats to small domestic ones. Even though they may look quite different, all cats share the same common "language" through scent, sight, sound, and touch.

Masters of understatement

Cats also use sounds and signals to communicate with one another and with us, but these are quite subtle in comparison to dogs or humans. For example, when two people meet for the first time they will usually smile, raise their eyebrows in greeting, and shake hands. Two cats meeting for the first time may look as though they are completely disinterested in each other, because they are likely to keep completely still and only blink an eye or twitch an ear in communication.

What do you think this cat is saying?

CAT FACT
It is thought that a cat's vision is 10 times less effective than a person's. However, they have 200 million odor-sensitive cells in their noses. Humans only have five million!

Complete strangers or best of friends? Cat language is subtle.

Think cat

Cats must regard some of our habits as very strange! Although cats enjoy affection and physical contact, they never hug each other, so for us to try and cuddle them must be rather bewildering! Perhaps it's no wonder that some cats can be wary of people. Just imagine what it must be like for a cat to meet someone using crutches for the first time!

Try to think about life from your cat's point of view. Imagine what it must be like to be so much smaller than us, but also more agile and sensitive. It must be confusing at times!

Cat language: Tail, body, legs, and feet

Feline body language is subtle. This means you need to be good at watching for small movements and tiny signals to understand what your cat is feeling. Look closely at the different parts of her body and how she moves them to express herself.

Overall body posture

Look at your cat's body. Is it relaxed or tense? Cats that are feeling anxious tend to hunch their backs and make themselves look as small as possible. They may stay very still and move only their eyes and ears to keep watch. Cats that are relaxed will stretch themselves out and tend to move in a calm, unhurried way.

Tails up!

Cats use their tails to tell us how they feel. It is easy to spot when your cat is happy to see you. She will come toward you with her tail held straight up in the air and just the tip bent over. A calm cat may move about with her tail held down, hanging in a relaxed fashion.

A cat that is angry or thinking about pouncing may swish her tail gently from side to side or twitch the tip. A tail thrashing from side to side is definitely a warning that the cat is either very excited or aggressive. You are most likely to see this if your cat is watching birds out of the window and is frustrated that she can't reach them!

Crazy kitten tails

Kittens sometimes hold their tails in an unusual, upside-down U shape. This shows that they are being playful and full of fun. It's most often seen when a kitten is having a wild game and suddenly dashes around the room in a strange sideways step.

Perfectly adapted for hunting, your cat's paws are an exceptional piece of feline engineering.

Paws for thought

Your cat's feet are brilliantly designed! The claws can be retracted, which means that they can be pulled up out of the way during normal walking and running, but can be immediately produced as weapons when hunting or fighting. Their claws are very sharp and strong and are curved to hook into prey and hold on to it.

Threat response

Cats that are feeling angry or very frightened may hold their tails bolt upright and fluff them up in a characteristic "bottle brush" pose. They do this so that their tails look as big as possible to try to frighten off a threat, such as another cat or a dog.

A cat's "righting reflex" can save her from injury or even death if she falls.

CAT FACT

The domestic cat is the only cat species able to hold its tail vertically while walking. All wildcats, such as lions, tigers, and leopards, hold their tails horizontally or tucked between their legs when they walk.

Right on!

Cats' movements are lithe, graceful, and athletic. They can turn and twist far better than many other animals because they have a very flexible spine and no collarbone. This allows them to right themselves even in midair, which prevents them from being hurt during a fall by allowing them to fall on their feet. Kittens develop this ability—known as the "righting reflex"—by the time they are only seven weeks old.

Cat language: Head, ears, and mouth

Cats' faces are simply beautiful. With their remarkable eyes, their stunning markings, and their amazing whiskers, it's little wonder that so many pictures of cats make it onto our walls! As well as being lovely to look at, a cat's face holds important clues to what she is feeling.

Eyes

A cat's eyes can give you a lot of information about how the cat is feeling, but you do need to know how to "read" them. A cat can narrow her eyes into thin slits or open them wide in a stare, which makes them very expressive.

A cat that is relaxed and content will half close or narrow her eyes. She may blink very slowly and turn her face away from you. This is not an insult, but shows instead that she is happy in your company!

CAT FACT

Some cats may not be able to express themselves in the same way if they have long hair or belong to a certain breed. Persian cats have flattened faces, which means they are unable to move their whiskers. Sphynx cats are hairless and usually have no whiskers at all!

The perfect picture of contentment!

Humans tend to use direct eye contact when they are speaking, which can be interpreted as a threat by cats if they do not know you.

Cats that are fearful will usually have eyes that are wide open. Their pupils—the black circles in the center of their eyes—will often dilate, which means they become larger. Angry cats may also have wide eyes, but the pupils will narrow to thin, vertical slits.

Whiskers

A cat's whiskers are highly mobile and can be moved to point forward when they are hunting. This is thought to help the cat locate the exact position of their prey by picking up vibrations sent through their whiskers.

This cat's magnificent whiskers emphasize her expressions perfectly.

Relaxed cats usually hold their ears facing forward and tilted back slightly. If something interests them, their ears tend to prick up slightly, to catch the sound. Angry cats may rotate their ears so that the insides face to the side and the backs of the ears face forward. This is a clear signal to back off! Frightened cats flatten their ears so that they lie against their heads. This gives the head a sleek appearance and means that the cat is preparing for "fight or flight": to either attack or run away.

A relaxed cat holds her whiskers outwards in a natural "fan," while a cat that is excited, tense, or angry may also point her whiskers out, but hold them fanned widely open.

Ears

Domestic cats' ears are nearly all the same size and shape, no matter what the breed or type, and they are highly expressive. Thirty different muscles allow the ears to turn left and right, as well as move backward and forward. Cats' ears can also move independently of each other, so one can swivel one way while the other does the opposite!

Ear positions can express anxiety, fear, interest, and even anger.

CAT FACT

A cat's sense of hearing is very acute and much better than a person's. The shape of a cat's ear is designed to channel sound into the ear canal, so they can hear the tiny, high-pitched sounds of prey animals, like mice, several yards away. Your cat's sensitive hearing may put her off from sitting too close to the TV or stereo when the volume is high.

Cat language: Scent

Cats have a very sensitive sense of smell. This is useful for finding prey, but is also an essential part of their communication system.

In the wild, cats would usually live separate from one another. They communicate long-distance in order to avoid confrontations, leaving scent signals for one another by rubbing, scratching, and depositing urine and feces.

Cats can recognize one another by the way they smell. They can do this with such accuracy that they can tell who's been in their neighborhood, at what time, and for how long! All this information can be gained by sniffing a place where another cat has left a scent signal.

Cats sometimes squirt urine to leave an odor message for other cats. This is called "spraying."

Cats usually bury their feces, unless they wish to leave a very obvious signal on show!

Rubbing

All cats have scent glands in their heads and faces, as well as at the base of their tails and paws. These glands release a chemical combination that is unique to that cat—a bit like how a fingerprint is unique to a human being. This individual scent helps make the cat feel secure and comfortable. For this reason they like to replenish the smell by rubbing frequently on surfaces in the home as well as on us! This makes us smell familiar so we are easily recognized by our cats. When the family all smell the same, the scent is referred to as the "clan odor."

Scratching

Cats use scratching to leave a visual signal as well as a scent signal. People who have had a cat scratch their furniture know what the visual signal looks like! Scratching releases scent from between the cat's pads onto the surface being scratched. Although humans cannot detect this scent, to another cat it must be like reading someone's online profile on a Web page.

This type of marking is natural for cats, but infuriating for humans!

Urine

Special chemicals in cats' urine act as messages, which other cats can "read." To make sure these messages get noticed, cats spray urine in a very specific way, so that it lands at cat-nose height! Although it's normal for all cats—both male and female, neutered and not—to mark like this outdoors, unfortunately cats that are anxious or stressed may choose to spray inside as well.

Feces

Although cats usually bury their waste by covering it with soil, they will sometimes leave visual and smelly messages by leaving their feces out on display. This must be the equivalent of displaying a message on a giant billboard!

Welcome home!

Your cat may give you a little hoplike greeting by bumping against your leg, quickly lifting both front paws off the ground, then putting them back. This is a version of a greeting she learned from her mother. Cats head-rub and nose-rub to say hello and to mingle scents. People are too tall for that, so cats settle for what they can reach!

CAT FACT

Every cat has its own individual scent, like a feline fingerprint. Some drugs, such as antibiotics, can alter this unique smell temporarily. This means that two cats may not recognize each other if one has been given medication at the vet's office. To avoid this, keep the two cats apart for a short while after you return home from the vet. Stroke one cat and encourage her to rub against you, then immediately go and stroke the other. This rebuilds the clan odor before the two cats meet each other again.

Cat language: Using scent signals with your cat

Understanding that your cat communicates via smell is very important. Humans are not particularly tuned in to this way of "speaking" so we have to make a conscious effort to help our cats feel comfortable by using scent signals around the home.

Most cats like to rub their heads, bodies, and tails on us to transfer their scent.

Family bonds

First and foremost, it is very important that you and your cat smell alike! Cats feel comfortable and secure when their family smells familiar, which is why they like to rub on us to share their scent. This leaves a trace of their own individual scent behind. We cannot see or smell this, but it is essential for your cat to feel comfortable with you and the home. Of course, humans wash their hands with soap and use perfumes and deodorants, which must be quite overwhelming for our cats. They need to keep replenishing their efforts to make us smell the same!

To encourage your cat to rub her face and chin on your hands, make sure that you wait for her to approach you. It is bad cat manners to approach her, and your cat may be distressed if you try to force her to rub against you, so sit quietly and allow your hand to hang down. See if she rubs your hand or arm. If she does, you can gently stroke behind her ears and around her face, as this will help to spread her scent. Some timid cats prefer to rub against your legs. Most cats will do this when they are hungry.

Your cat rubs on you to ensure you have a shared "clan odor."

Scent trick

In order to make sure that your cat accepts new items in the house, you can trick her into thinking that she has seen them before!

1 Take a clean cloth, such as a napkin.

2 Encourage your cat to rub her face on the cloth by holding it in your hand. Don't be tempted to wipe it on her face. She must volunteer the behavior.

3 As soon as she has rubbed on the cloth you can wipe it on the new article or piece of furniture. Humans cannot see or smell this signal, but the new item will now seem familiar to your cat. This should prevent her from marking it in another way, such as by scratching it!

Part of the furniture

To make sure that this comforting and familiar scent is constantly around her, your cat will most likely rub every day. Most cats have favorite places to do this—against the edge of the sofa, for example, or the bottom step of the stairs. Although they might leave some hairs behind, this kind of marking is harmless to us and to our furniture!

Sensitive cats might find new furniture and other new things in the home quite upsetting. This is because they look and, more importantly, smell unfamiliar. They might try to mark the object in other ways, such as by scratching it or even by spraying urine on it.

Rubbing new furniture with a "scent cloth" can help your cat feel at home.

Cat language: Vocalizations

Although cats have more limited communication signals than dogs or people, when communicating close up, they do use a range of sounds to show how they are feeling. Many cats learn to vary the pitch and frequency of the sounds they make in response to the attention we give them. Some are so good at this that it can sound as though they are "talking"!

Purring

The ultimate sound that signals contentment, peace, and harmony: Purring is the sound cats make when they are truly content. This behavior starts very early in a cat's life. Kittens purr when they are feeding from their mother to let her know that they are content.

Cats keep their mouths closed when they purr, and can purr without stopping as they breathe in and out! It is thought that this sound is generated by vibrations in their vocal cords, which are structured in a way that is unique to cats!

Complete contentment! You can almost hear this kitten purr!

Meowing

Cats can't communicate by using words, but they can still train humans to do what they want by making certain sounds. Your cat may meow, mew, chirrup, screech, or even sing! Most "talking" sounds are made when cats open their mouths to make a sound and then close it again at the end. If you listen to your cat and watch her behavior, you will start to notice that certain sounds may become associated with particular actions. Some owners have managed to distinguish at least sixteen different sounds that their cat makes. Each can have a different meaning, such as "Let me in," "Let me out," "Give me food," "Pet me!" and "Where have you been?"

CAT FACT
Lions do occasionally purr, but, unlike domestic cats, they do not use purring as part of their social life. Instead of purring continuously, the way our cats do, lions only make a sound as they exhale. Large cats are divided into two groups: those that roar, such as tigers and African lions, and those that purr. Mountain lions purr, hiss, scream, and snarl, but they cannot roar!

TRY THIS AT HOME
Why not try recording your cat's sounds? Play them back and analyze what they might mean to become really proficient in cat language!

Yowling

Some cats also yowl. This is a long sound that the cat makes by opening her mouth, then closing it slightly to alter the tone of her voice. Yowling is usually designed to get attention. If owners aren't careful, it can become a bit of a habit! A "song" may be nice to hear during the day, but doesn't sound so good in the middle of the night when you are trying to sleep.

Some breeds of cat, such as Siamese cats, are more vocal than others. They like to "talk" to their owners all the time and may become loud and demanding if they are ignored!

**Beware! This cat is clearly saying
"Go away!" with both visual and
sound signals!**

Hissing and growling

Cats hiss when they are trying to defend themselves. The cat will open her mouth halfway, draw back her upper lip, and wrinkle her face. As she does this, she expels a jet of air. Sometimes the moisture she releases with this air also comes out as a jet. This is referred to as spitting and can be effective in driving off even large animals. Perhaps it looks or sounds a little like a snake attacking!

Cats can also growl. The growling sound is made deep in the back of the cat's throat, and is a clear warning to keep away.

**Many cats learn to make sounds that their
owners can translate, such as "Feed me!"**

How to read your cat's emotions

Like us, cats can be happy, sad, angry, and content. They can feel playful or sleepy, independent or cuddly. In order to have the best possible relationship with your cat, it's important to learn to recognize her emotions and respond to them accordingly.

Imagine if your best friend at school were feeling sad—you would know even without their telling you. Their face and their body language would give you clues.

Quiet charms

Understanding how your cat is feeling takes a little time and patience. Cats don't speak

Dogs use more obvious communication signals than cats—but they can still learn to "read" each other!

English, so they cannot tell us how they feel. Cats are also very different from dogs. They are not truly a social species as dogs are, which means that they use less obvious signals to express themselves.

When a dog is happy and excited, he may run towards you, wagging his tail and looking up at you with bright eyes and a soft expression. He may whine or bark in excitement and may bring you a toy to play with. When a cat is happy and pleased to see you, she may walk slowly towards you, raise her tail, then give you a gentle rub with her chin!

Because cats are very subtle in the way that they communicate, many people do not take the time to learn to understand them. They may stroke a cat, but not notice that her ears are back and her eyes are wide—both are signals that she's not really enjoying it.

Long-distance communication

Understanding that cats like to use long-distance communication is the first step in being able to "read" their emotions. In a wild situation, cats would use

Alert and inquisitive, this cat is keen to approach.

steps to make sure she feels safe and comfortable. If she's feeling playful and friendly, you will know just how to play with her. If she's feeling content and sleepy, you can recognize that mood and enjoy it, too.

Cats are often thought of as mysterious and even secretive. Learning how to recognize and understand your cat will make you part of an exclusive group of people who can truly "speak cat"!

scent the way we might send a group email—to announce their presence to other cats. This message would be "read" long before the cats actually set eyes on one another.

Cats live in a world of scent that humans often fail to understand, because our sense of smell isn't very sensitive. We all know what it's like to be bombarded with color or loud noises. For cats, being bombarded with smells must be somewhat similar. Just imagine what it must be like for a cat to be taken to the vet. The smells of other animals, people, cleaning products, and even perfume, must be almost overwhelming. It's little wonder that hardly any cats look or feel relaxed at the vet's!

Reach a comfortable understanding

Learning to understand how your cat is feeling is one of the most important aspects of your relationship with her. If you can tell whether she is feeling frightened, anxious, or worried, you can take

Learn cat language and discover what your cat really likes in life.

How your cat says "I'm scared!"

Cats enjoy being sociable with people and other animals that they know, but can easily become scared of unfamiliar sights, sounds, and smells. This is a sensible survival strategy to keep them out of danger. Cats nearly always prefer to run away or hide if they are frightened, rather than fight. Many of their body language signals when they are frightened show that they are preparing to escape.

The first signs

Cats are usually quiet when they are anxious, which means they may not appear to be worried until they actually run away. If you are good at spotting the early warning signs that your cat is anxious, you can give her space and help her feel more confident. You can protect her in the same way that an older brother or sister might!

Ears turned away and held back, eyes wide and staring, body tense and rigid. This cat is clearly anxious.

Sit tight

The first sign that your cat is feeling concerned might simply be that she sits still, or, if she's being held, that she leans away from you. She may look hunched in an attempt to make herself smaller. Her ears may be flattened to her head, and her eyes wide and staring. Cats that are very worried may have dilated pupils. Her whiskers may also be pulled back and she is likely to hold her tail down low—again, to avoid attracting attention.

Escape

As soon as a frightened cat feels that it is safe enough, she is likely to try to escape. Often she will try to slink away with her body low to the ground and her legs crouching. She may move slowly, sometimes just one paw at a time, in an attempt to get away without anyone noticing. She will then look for somewhere to hide—perhaps under a bed or behind a building or large object. She will be prepared to sit still, sometimes for many hours, until she feels safe enough to venture out.

If a frightened cat can't see a place to hide, she may run. Her escape route might be out of a door or window or to a high point such as up a tree or on top of a cupboard or door.

How to help

It is usually best to try to remove the source of your cat's fear rather than try to comfort her directly. Don't try to hold her, cuddle her, or pick her up if she looks scared. This may cause her to panic and scratch you in an attempt to get away.

Even though she might have been enjoying contact at first, this cat has decided it's time to escape!

Boxed in

It may seem odd to us, but cats feel safe when they are in small, enclosed spaces. For this reason they sometimes like hiding in cupboards or even in bags! If you think your cat is worried about something, you can give her a small space to hide in. Pyramid cat beds are wonderful for this, or you can use a cardboard box covered with a blanket.

Anger—what are the signs?

Although most cats, when faced with a threat, would rather run away than become aggressive, occasionally cats can become frustrated or angry. Learning feline body language for anger is important. It means you can avoid getting hurt or upsetting your cat further.

Silent confrontation

As they are with their other emotions, cats are quite subtle in showing annoyance and we need to look carefully to understand what they are saying. Two cats having a confrontation may never actually make physical contact. They may simply have a staring match until one cat wins!

Tell-tail signs

One of the ways of telling when a cat is feeling mildly annoyed or frustrated is to watch her tail. If you see the tip twitching, it is likely that the cat is feeling a little frustrated. If her whole tail swishes from side to side and her ears are twitching, these are signs that her annoyance is increasing. If it thrashes from side to side, watch out—she's really cross!

This cat is showing subtle signs of annoyance. The tail is twitching, her ears are back, and she looks tense. Exercise caution!

Beware!

A cat that is angry and feeling confident will often have narrowed pupils. Her whiskers may be pushed forwards and her ears may be swiveled around so that the backs are visible from the front. Her hackles may go up, which raises her hair all over her body to make her look bigger than she really is, and her tail may become so fluffed up that it is described as being "bottle brush." She may also turn sideways to emphasize her size and to try to scare off her attacker.

Cats can also arch their backs to make themselves look bigger. This is a really impressive movement. They can extend like this because their spines contain nearly 60 vertebrae, which fit loosely together and give them incredible flexibility. Humans only have 34 vertebrae in comparison.

Cats showing these sorts of postures are clearly not going to back down. They will swipe with their claws extended if the threat comes any closer!

Cats would always rather run than fight, but they will defend themselves if they feel cornered.

No pushover

An angry or defensive cat may sometimes roll over onto her back. It might look like she is being cute or "appeasing" (trying to look like she is no threat), but in fact the opposite is true. A cat on its back like this is getting ready to use all her claws and teeth to defend herself if necessary. Cats will also roll over in play, or to get attention, but their body language looks quite different in these circumstances.

CAT FACT

Cats have four very long teeth at the fronts of their mouths. These look like fangs, but are really called "canine teeth." They use these to catch and kill prey—this is why they are sharp and strong. When a cat bites, it transfers lots of germs and bacteria into the wound. This can cause serious infections, so if your cat bites you, you will need to see a doctor.

Full, direct eye contact or staring is a clear warning signal here.

How to tell if your cat is happy

You can almost see the smile on a truly contented cat's face! Curled up on your lap or snoozing in her favorite spot in the sun, a contented cat sometimes draws the corners of her mouth upwards in a gentle grin!

Greet me

A happy and confident cat will walk straight towards you, tail up in the air. She will often want to rub on you or may even push her face towards yours and engage in a head rub if she can reach you. This is a clear friendship greeting!

CAT FACT

We all know that purring indicates a cat is happy, don't we? Well, yes and no. Cats do purr—often very loudly—when they are content. However, they are also known to purr when extremely frightened or in pain, so it is thought that purring is really an expression of intense emotion.

Happy and relaxed, with eyes half closed, this cat is clearly very comfortable.

A cat that is trying to get your attention and show she is friendly will sometimes jump up onto a high surface, such as the sofa or a wall, and may parade backwards and forwards, rubbing on things as she goes, and purring loudly. This is an invitation to approach, and as soon as you do, the cat will go into a frenzy of head and cheek rubbing. This type of confident cat may also position herself under your hand, so that you are effectively forced to stroke her all the way down her back and tail!

**Kittens are full of fun—
and their body language
shows it!**

Close to you

Happy cats love getting close to people who they know. They feel secure snuggled up to you and will often fold their paws underneath their bodies, and purr loudly. Cats are really divided into two camps when it comes to close physical contact with people: those that like to sit on laps and those that don't! Some lap cats are so keen to make themselves at home on your knee that you have barely sat down before they jump on and make themselves comfortable. Other cats, which tend to be slightly more aloof characters, enjoy having contact, but with a slight distance. Typically, these cats just love sitting next to you on the sofa, and will often stretch out one paw and place that on your knee or hand, just to feel your closeness. Both sorts of cats are showing affection and contentment In their own way, so it's best to accept them as they are rather than try to change them.

CAT FACT

Happy kittens often have a very specific, and unusual, way of letting off steam. They arch their backs, and then run in an odd sideways stepping movement, which looks a bit like disco dancing! They also hold their tails in a characteristic loop —like an inverted U.

Wild cat vs tame kitten

When your cat is outside, or indoors playing, she is a brave hunter, wild and free. However, once she is on your lap, she shows her domestic side—which is all about the inner kitten! When content and safe indoors, cats seem to revert to kittenhood, and treat us like Mom. If your cat likes to climb on you, then starts kneading you with her paws and dribbling like a baby, it's a sure sign that she's supremely happy. This behavior is a copy of what she used to do as a kitten to stimulate her mother to give her milk—she's doing just the same to us!

How to have a "conversation" with your cat

The best way of inviting your cat to have a conversation with you is to sit and do nothing! This is because most cats are tempted to go towards people who are quiet and who don't try to approach them.

Small talk

This is how you send an invitation to chat.

1 Sit quietly on a sofa or the floor. Make sure the area is calm and quiet.

2 As your cat approaches, turn your face to one side.

3 Avert your eyes so that you are not looking directly at your cat.

4 Dangle your hand down. Once your cat has made contact by touching or rubbing your hand, you can gently stroke around her head and ears.

5 If she's enjoying this, you can run your hand down her back and all the way up her tail.

Having a conversation with your cat will strengthen your relationship with her.

Shy cat help

By now, you should be good at noticing when your cat is contented and relaxed and when she would most enjoy company and contact. If your cat is slightly nervous or doesn't like having close contact with people, don't try to force her. Instead, use mealtimes as a way into her heart. Talk to her gently while you prepare her food, and feed her on a high surface so she feels safe. Many cats enjoy being stroked while they eat. This can be a good way of forging a friendship with your cat without creating any anxiety. Feeding her lots of tiny meals instead of fewer, larger portions will give you more opportunities to pet her, too.

Deep in conversation

Once your cat is confident, you may find that she jumps up onto the sofa next to you or into your lap so that she is closer to your face. Now the conversation can really begin!

1 As your cat looks at you, turn your face away a little and half close your eyes.

2 You can make little kissing sounds with your mouth while you stroke her.

3 Watch your cat out of the corner of your eye. When you notice that she turns her face away from yours, you can look back towards her again.

4 See if you can have a two-way conversation with your facial expression and eye contact—each time your cat turns her face away and narrows her eyes, you can mirror this and do the same in turn.

Cats often approach people who are ignoring them—this is because their body language appears to be nonthreatening.

Roll over

Cats sometimes roll on their backs on the floor for attention. This looks a bit doglike, but don't be fooled. It may look as though your cat is inviting you to tickle her tummy, but, while some cats like this in small doses, others hate it and will lash out at your hand with their claws or teeth. Whether your cat likes or dislikes having her tummy tickled is very individual. You had better ask an adult to find out first!

TOP TIPS

🐾 Give short but frequent sessions of attention to your cat. This means she will look forward to each one.

🐾 Talk quietly to your cat. Don't shout or make a sudden loud noise, as this will scare her.

🐾 Keep fairly still while you interact with your cat. Sudden movements can be off-putting.

🐾 Always allow your cat to come to you. Never chase her or pester her for attention.

Rolling over may look cute, but beware of those claws!

Cat-speak quiz

Check out the pictures and see if you can tell what each cat is "saying"! Choose option a, b, or c for each picture, then add up your score to find out how well you can speak cat!

1

- (a) I'm frightened.
- (b) I'm blissfully content to be with you.
- (c) I'm playful—please pet me.

2

- (a) I'm bored.
- (b) I'm angry— keep away.
- (c) Hello—nice to meet you!

3

- (a) I don't really like this.
- (b) I'm perfectly happy.
- (c) I'm enjoying this cuddle.

4

- (a) I've got an itch.
- (b) I'm asking you to play
- (c) I like you and I want to transfer my scent onto your hand.

5
- **a** Keep back, I'm in a bad mood.
- **b** I want your attention!
- **c** I'm just exercising.

6
- **a** Come and pet me, please!
- **b** I feel threatened— go away!
- **c** I'm just thinking about what's for lunch.

7
- **a** I love talking with you.
- **b** I'm going to bite you!
- **c** I'm not sure about you yet.

8
- **a** Hello! Lovely to see you! Please pet me.
- **b** I'm busy, leave me alone.
- **c** I'm scared and want to run away.

Your score:
1–2 correct: More practice required. Try again!
3–4 correct: Good. Keep watching your cat!
5–6 correct: Very good. You can speak "feline" well.
7–8 out of 8: Excellent! You are a cat language expert!

Answers:
1. b, 2. c, 3. a, 4. c, 5. b, 6. b, 7. a, 8. c

How to Speak Cat

Did you know that a cat's brain is regarded as relatively large? A cat's brain is thought to be proportionally as large as a dolphin's. It is not known whether this means that cats are more intelligent than other animals of a similar size, because it is difficult to define intelligence in animals. Certainly, cats can learn. They can solve puzzles and can learn by association how to get the things they want in life and avoid things they don't like.

As any owner will tell you, cats also seem to have good memories and can remember people, events, and associations for long periods. You only have to get the flea spray out and most cats will disappear!

Learning how to make the most of your cat's intelligence with training will need an understanding of how she learns and what motivates her. It is almost impossible to force a cat to do something she doesn't want to do, especially for a second time, which is why certain tasks, such as giving your cat a pill, can be so difficult. Take the time to make training for your cat fun and successful. She will love you for it!

Start training your kitten as soon as possible—after all, it's much easier to learn a foreign language when you are 5 than 55!

What cats think about training

The art of training your cat is in encouraging her to perform a certain behavior because she wants to, not because you force her. Your cat will hide from you or may even run away if she doesn't enjoy her training, so make sure there are always rewards on offer, and prepare to be patient to get the result you want.

Star potential

Cats can be trained to perform almost any task they are physically capable of. They have been trained to run through play tunnels, open cupboard doors, lie down, crawl, and even meow on command. Some of the best-trained cats can become stars by appearing in commercials, on TV shows, or in films. Teaching your cat to perform simple tricks is fun and can help develop the trust between you. It can also be useful: Just imagine if your cat would sit and stay so that you could take a photo of her!

Work to her strengths

No matter what you are hoping to teach your cat to do, she must always think that it was her idea. Think about what kinds of natural behaviors your cat already displays, and how you could put them to use. Perhaps your cat likes to roll on her back. All you'd need to do would be to reward this behavior each time she did it with a treat or a game. Once she's rolling on her back consistently in

Most cats will work for tidbits of food, but make sure they are really tasty.

Once you have been living with a cat for a while, it becomes obvious that it is not the cat being trained most of the time! Cats are masters at training us to do exactly what they want us to. This is not because they are trying to dominate us, but simply because they are very persistent in getting what they want.

Your cat will tell you when she's had enough! Never try to force her to do training.

> ## CAT FACT
> Some cats learn to wake their owners at a certain time every morning (or in the middle of the night, if their owners are very unlucky). Others train their owners to feed them whenever they meow near the fridge! This behavior might be cute to begin with, but after a while it can become annoying, so it's always best to be aware of which habits you are rewarding.

the hopes of a reward, you could attach a command to the behavior, such as "Roll over," and ask her to do it when you want her to, not just when she does.

Valuable training

Some people may think that it's a little strange to train your cat to sit or come when called, but training can improve your cat's quality of life by exercising her brain as well as her body, especially if she lives indoors. It can also help to keep her safe, allowing you to call her away from danger or find out where she is, for example. Some humans may think of tricks as a little frivolous, but to your cat they are a good way of spending quality time with her best friend—with some treats thrown in for free!

Most of the time cats are clever enough to train us!

Rewards, rewards, rewards!

We all know that the chance of getting a reward can make us work harder. Just think about how much more effort you might put in if you knew that you would get a shiny new bike or iPod for passing an exam, or how much keener you might be to tidy your bedroom if you thought a special treat was being offered!

Make it tasty

Cats are the same. Just like us, cats need to know that there's something worth working for, and it needs to be something they would choose for themselves. While most dogs will jump through hoops to get a biscuit, many cats will wrinkle their noses in disgust at the idea of eating a dry, boring piece of cat food. A pat on the head is about as welcome for your cat as a bowl of cabbage would be for you! Yuck!

Getting it right

Tiny pieces of cooked chicken, flakes of cooked fish, such as tuna, or even tiny bits of cheese can be tempting. Beware of using cooked liver, however, which may not be good for your cat's health if she eats too much of it. To be perfect, the treats you use need to be at room temperature. Make sure they are cut into tiny pieces no bigger than a pea—that way you can use several without filling your cat up.

A balanced diet

If you usually feed your cat by filling up her dish when it becomes empty, you may need to restrict the amount of food she gets in one day. This way she will want the treats that you offer during training. When training, always use food different from what your cat eats as dinner. Training treats need to be regarded as special.

Boring! Learn what your cat likes and use this knowledge when you reward her.

What's your type?

There's no doubt that some cats are easier to train than others. If your cat likes most foods, that will certainly help, as trying to tempt a fussy cat with treats can be difficult. Your cat's personality will also make a difference during training. Some cats are highly sociable, outgoing, and confident. These cats are less distracted by their environment than a cat that is a little insecure. Traits like these tend to be inherited from your cat's parents and cannot be changed, so you need to accept her as she is.

Start young

If you have a kitten, make sure you get started on her training as early as possible. Encouraging her to follow your hand when there is a treat clasped inside it or asking her to sit for a reward will kick-start her "career" in training and simplify the learning process later on.

Patting

Although most cats enjoy being stroked and petted, it's very bad manners to pat a cat on the head. Most cats don't enjoy it at all. This is not surprising if you think about it from their point of view. Suddenly a large hand arrives from above—it must seem rather threatening and a bit frightening.

Most cats love to play, so games make excellent rewards!

TOP TIP

Is your cat doing something you don't like to get your attention? Ignore the behavior and she'll give it up. Look at her, talk to her, or touch her, and she'll keep doing it.

Lessons for life

Cats have changed very little from their ancestors, who lived many centuries ago. It is thought that they are no different genetically from the African wildcat— their ancient relative. So how is it that this "wild" animal can enjoy curling up and sleeping on our beds?

Getting out and about

All cats need to have lots of practice meeting and being with humans while they are still very young. They have to learn to cope with the sights, sounds, and smells of our human world before they develop a fear of new people, places, or experiences. The more people your cat can meet and mix with while she is young, the better, so make sure you fill her social diary! See the opposite page for ideas.

Be careful with me! This little kitten is well supported.

Pick your kitten up safely

Your kitten should feel safe and secure when you or other people pick her up. Put one hand under her chest and use the other to support her rear end. Hold your kitten close to your chest, so she feels stable. If your kitten is very squirmy, it is best to ask an adult to help you by lifting her onto your lap so that you can stroke her. Be careful when you put your kitten back on the floor. Sometimes cats will try to jump when they see the ground. You might get scratched if this happens!

Try to look at your kitten and see the future. Don't allow her to do things now that you won't like later on!

Correct stroking

When meeting new people, cats nearly always prefer to make the first move, rather than be approached. It's often best to ask your friends to sit down and pretend that they are ignoring your cat to begin with. You'll soon find that she comes trotting up to be nosy! Once she has approached, they can stroke her by tickling her around the ears and stroking along her back in the direction that the hair is growing.

You will easily be able to tell if your kitten is enjoying this. Most cats purr like an engine when they are enjoying being petted, and simply put their tails in the air and walk away if they aren't!

Ask your friends to be gentle with your kitten so that she learns to like new people.

Your cat's social diary

Your cat's age	Social must-dos!
2–7 weeks	This is the most critical time in your kitten's social development. She is learning to be a cat and discovering that people are friendly and nice to be with. While she's still with the breeder, it's vital that your kitten is regularly handled by at least four people, and introduced to a domestic environment.
7–12 weeks	When your kitten comes home, she needs to meet people of as many different ages, sizes, and shapes as possible! Invite your friends over and make sure she has a lovely time being petted and played with every day. If your kitten is confident and outgoing, why not hold a kitten party so everyone can meet her? Also, make sure she hears and sees lots of different everyday occurrences, such as the washing machine on its spin cycle and the floor being vacuumed.
12 weeks–6 months	It's important that your kitten keeps up with her social engagements and continues to meet lots of people who will hold her, stroke her, and talk to her. This way she will be friendly with new people, not frightened or aggressive.

Making friends at home

You would rather not argue with your family. Cats would prefer to live in a peaceful household, too! So long as your pets are properly introduced, have enough space, and all receive enough at mealtimes, there is no reason they can't be happy housemates!

It's essential that your kitten gets used to all of the other animals she will be living with.

Reigning cats and dogs

It's a myth that cats and dogs don't get along well together. Given lots of early training and plenty of opportunities to get used to each other, they should have no problems becoming best buddies. However, first impressions do count, so it's important to plan how your kitten is going to meet your dog.

To introduce your kitten to your dog, make sure that she feels safe by allowing her to sit somewhere up high or by keeping her in a carrying basket to begin with, so that they can both smell each other first.

Dogs and cats can be great friends, but first impressions count!

Overenthusiastic dogs

It's important to be realistic about whether your dog is generally friendly towards other animals and whether his training is up to standard. If you are concerned that he might chase your new kitten or hurt her, keep him on a leash to begin with. If he seems obsessed with the kitten or gets excited, it may be best to ask a dog trainer to help you.

Cat to cat

Although some cats enjoy the company of other cats in the same household, they are not truly a social species. If you want to have more than one cat at home, ensure that there are plenty of warm and comfy resting places, feeding dishes, and litter boxes so every cat feels that she has her rightful share!

Other pets

If your kitten is going to live with other pets, such as rabbits, it's important that she learns to be friends with them early on. If you are unsure how the animals will react to one another, use carrying cages or pens to begin with.

Polite introductions

In the wild, one cat would introduce itself to another by leaving scent messages long before they saw each other face to face. You can re-create this system by making sure that your adult cat gets used to the smell of your kitten before they actually meet.

1 When you bring your kitten home, take her to a room different from the one your adult cat is in. Spend time stroking her and making her feel at home, then go and stroke your adult cat. Rub your hands on the furniture around the rest of the house, too. This will accustom your adult cat to your new kitten's smell.

2 After a day or two, when your kitten has settled in, you can take her into another room and then take your older cat into the room where your kitten has been. Allow them both lots of time to explore and feel relaxed and comfortable on their own.

3 For the first face-to-face meeting, it is often best to keep your new kitten contained in a carrying cage or indoor pen. This allows the cats to see and smell each other without being frightened. It's very important that you do not allow your kitten to run away, as this can trigger the older cat to chase her—not a good start to a friendship!

4 Feed your kitten in the pen or cage and feed your adult cat a small amount of very tasty food at the same time, a little distance apart. Do this several times, because it helps both cats to think nice things about each other.

5 Finally, feed your two cats some distance apart, without the protective bars of the cage. Keep stroking one and then the other. They will build up a good "clan odor" and regard each other as family.

If your new kitten stays in a cage at first, both cats will feel more at ease.

Early learning: Manners and safe play

Good manners are essential for all the family. Your cat is no exception. Many behavioral problems can be prevented if you teach your kitten to be polite and to play nicely without using teeth or claws.

Play safe

Unfortunately, many people look at a cute, cuddly kitten and just can't resist playing with them, allowing the kitten to chase their hands or feet, or using their hands to "wrestle" with the kitten. These kinds of games teach the kitten that it's okay to use her teeth and claws when playing, which might be harmless when she's young, but will hurt when she gets older! Avoid any kind of play fighting with your cat. Although it may start out as fun, cats can suddenly become frightened and may lash out.

Never allow your kitten to bite or hang off your hair or clothes. Either play fetch games instead or use long toys, which keep your hands well out of reach—wands and "fishing rod" type toys are perfect for this.

Master and servant

Many cats learn quickly that they can treat us like slaves! If they want food, they meow and we run to the cupboard. If they don't like what we give them, they turn up their noses and we rush to the supermarket to buy them something different! If you don't want your cat to call the shots later on, make sure you don't behave like a servant now!

Ball games are fun and don't encourage bad habits.

CAT MANNERS CHECKLIST:

Don't!

🐾 Play with your kitten by teasing her or wrestling with her.

🐾 Allow your kitten to chase or bite at your hands or feet.

🐾 Encourage your kitten to do things that will cause problems later on.

Do!

🐾 Play with your kitten often, using toys that keep your hands well out of the way.

🐾 Have calm times with your kitten, when you simply sit with her and read your book.

🐾 Handle your kitten a lot, using slow, gentle movements so that she feels comfortable with you.

How to ignore your kitten

Kittens are so cute that most humans (especially grown-ups!) need lessons in how to ignore them when they are pestering for attention. Ignoring your cat gives her the message that she won't get attention by being pushy. You only need to ignore her for a minute or two, but be consistent.

"Oops, I've been naughty": It's no fun to be ignored!

1 Fold your arms and turn your body away from your cat.

2 Avoid eye contact and don't speak to her or touch her.

3 Get up and leave the room as if you are disgusted by her behavior!

Don't do that!

The secret of making sure that your cat is well behaved is to try to think like she does. If you can see the world from your cat's point of view, you will suddenly realize that what seems naughty to us often looks like fun to her!

Biting

Biting can mean trouble for you and your cat. Although some cats start by biting gently in play, this can quickly become more dangerous if she bites hard and breaks the skin. Even if your cat is biting you gently, follow the guidelines below.

1 Immediately say "No" to your cat and stop playing.

2 Walk out of the room as though you are disgusted with her.

Biting and scratching must be stopped immediately— no exceptions.

It is very important that your cat understands that biting means the end of fun and games and will not be tolerated.

Pouncing

Some kittens will pounce on their owners during their "mad half hour" in the evenings. This rushing around seems to be an outlet for pent-up energy, but pouncing can become a bad habit if your cat learns to enjoy it.

If you can predict that your cat will pounce on you at a certain time, try to prevent it by playing a game with her using a wand or fishing rod type of toy, so that she can safely use up some energy! If your cat does suddenly spring at you, try not to give her attention. Follow the rules above for responding to biting.

Scratching furniture

Cats need to scratch! Normally they will do this on a tree or post outdoors—or indoors if there's one provided. Sometimes, however, cats take a fancy to scratching one particular piece of furniture.

To solve this problem, look at where the scratching is taking place. Is the furniture in line with a door or a window? Nearly always, scratching is intended as a message and indicates that they are feeling a little insecure.

If your kitten can explore in her own time, she is less likely to develop aggressive behavior.

The most common reason is that they are feeling anxious about their home being invaded, either by a cat or dog that already lives there or by cats or dogs that live nearby. The scratching message says, "I live here and these are my things."

Reduce feline anxiety

Try to make your cat feel more secure. If you think she's worried about something outside, keep the curtains or blinds closed and take your shoes off when you enter the house, as we sometimes bring the smells of other cats inside with us. Move the piece of furniture that is being scratched and encourage your cat to rub her face on it instead of scratching. This is a much better way of making her mark.

Getting onto work surfaces

From a feline point of view, work surfaces are excellent places to find food and shiny things to play with, and also provide good views out the window! From up there, they can look down on other cats or dogs and tease them safely!

For most cats, jumping or climbing onto work surfaces is fun and rewarding, until we catch them there. At this point they suddenly become frightened at our reaction—this doesn't stop them from repeating the behavior. It just makes them sneakier, and more likely to do it when we are not there!

If your kitten jumps up onto a table or a work surface and finds food that you have left there, it must be the equivalent of winning the kitty lottery! One good find like this and she will have learned that it's worth checking there every day. The only solution is to make sure you always tidy up after you have been preparing food. Always put tasty items away in a cupboard or out of reach when you are not there to supervise.

Feeding your cat in the same place every day will mean she's less likely to snoop!

Teaching cat-flap technique

If you are able to allow your cat free access to the outdoors, a cat flap can be very useful. This is like your cat's very own front door, allowing her to let herself in and out whenever she wants.

Outside in and inside out!

All cats need to learn how to use their doors. By following these instructions, you can help her learn quickly and easily.

1 To make it easy for your kitten or cat, prop open the flap using a lump of modeling clay or a piece of rolled up sticky tape wedged in the hinge. This will allow your kitten to look through the hole to the other side and not be frightened by the flap.

2 You will need a friend or an adult to help you with your kitten's training. Ask someone to hold your kitten gently outside the propped-open flap, while you encourage the kitten to come through the hole by luring her with a treat and calling her name. It's best to start by calling your cat inside through the door, as this will give her security. Give her a treat the instant she comes through the flap. Repeat this several times.

3 As soon as your cat is confident about going through from outdoors to indoors, you can then put her inside, go outside yourself, and reward her for stepping through her door in the other direction.

4 When your kitten is completely confident with walking in and out the hole, it is time to gradually lower the flap. Start by propping the flap open about halfway. Encourage your cat to push against the flap to reach you. Give her lots of rewards for reaching you on the other side. You can then lower the flap a bit more and practice again.

5 Your cat is finally ready to push her way through the fully lowered flap. Give her lots or encouragement and praise for being brave!

Prepare to train your cat by propping the flap open halfway.

Off-limits

Some people like to keep their cats in at night to keep them safe from traffic and other dangers. Your cat needs to understand that she cannot go through the flap when it is locked. Although we can see that the flap is locked in place, a cat may not understand why she cannot push the flap open when only minutes before she could!

Placing a "sign" next to or across the flap will teach your cat to associate that sign with the flap being shut and will not try to break out! The sign can be anything convenient—such as a piece of cloth hung up next to the flap, or a piece of wood placed across the exit. Your cat will soon learn that the signal means "NO EXIT" and will not even attempt to get out. You must be absolutely consistent in putting the signal up each and every time the flap is closed, however, and always remember to remove it when the flap is open again.

TOP TIP

It is very important that your kitten learns how to operate the cat flap in her own time, so never push your kitten through the flap or push her paws or head against the door in an attempt to show her what to do. You could put her off for life by frightening her in this way.

Your cat needs motivation: Some tasty tidbits and lots of encouragement will help her to get the idea.

Teaching your cat to use a scratching post

Scratching is normal and natural feline behavior. It doesn't sharpen the claws, as some people believe, but it does help keep them in good condition: The outer layer becomes old and needs to be shed to expose the new claw surface underneath.

Cats scratch to leave scent messages for other cats to "read."

Scratching out a message

Scratching is also an important part of cat communication. Cats have glands between the pads of their feet that release scent onto the surface where they scratch—messages that can be understood by other cats in the house, yard, or local area. Of course, scratching also leaves a visible mark. This emphasizes the cat's message, like underlining an important word in a sentence.

In a natural environment, cats usually like to scratch on tree trunks or other upright objects, as their messages can easily be seen and sniffed at by passing cats. Some cats also like to scratch horizontally, however, so you might need to provide both upright and flat scratching areas for your cat if you keep her indoors.

Shopping opportunity

Scratching posts come in many different sizes, heights, and colors. They are often built by covering a wooden post in sisal rope or carpet. The most important aspect for your cat is height. In the wild, a cat would normally scratch by sitting on its haunches and reaching up as high as possible with its front paws to scratch. From this, we can figure out that the post needs to be as tall as an adult cat standing on her hind legs.

Mega-stretch! Those amazing claws need to be kept in top condition.

From a human point of view, covering a scratching post with stylish carpet that fits in with our furnishings may seem like the best thing to do. However, it's important that your cat can tell the difference between her scratching post and the carpet itself, so choosing a different covering for the post is usually the best idea.

Scratch and sniff

To encourage your kitten or a new cat to use the scratching post, make sure it smells familiar. Put the post somewhere central in your home and then transfer some of your cat's own scent onto the post by stroking her along her head and back, and then immediately rubbing your hands on the post.

If your cat still doesn't pay any attention to the post and seems to prefer scratching a different surface, attract her by attaching lengths of string or a cat toy to the top of the post. This will tempt her to reach up and put her paws on the scratching post. You can then praise her and play with her to reward this behavior.

CAT FACT

Cats' feet are a remarkable piece of feline engineering! Their claws are retractable, which means that they can pull their claws right back into the foot when they are not needed so that the claws completely disappear from view and touch. Cats can then flex and extend them again when they need to use them for hunting or climbing. All members of the cat family, except the cheetah, have this amazing ability.

You can encourage your cat to use the scratching post by rubbing it with catnip—an herb that some cats find irresistible!

Coming when called

Did you know that you could train your cat? It may take a little more patience than training a dog, but it's great fun and your cat should enjoy it, too.

Essential training

Training your cat to come when called is vital for her safety. It is essential that she will come running to you when you call her so that you can always find her indoors and out! Most cats appear when they hear the sound of their food being prepared or even the fridge door being opened. If a fridge can train your cat to come when called, you can, too!

CAT FACT
Even if your cat isn't allowed outdoors, it's still a good idea to teach her to come when called. Cats love hiding. You may not be able to find her if she's tucked herself under a blanket, inside a cupboard, or on top of a doorway!

Starting out

Every time you are going to prepare your cat's food, call her to you. Do this even if she is standing right in front of you. Use her name, for example, "Molly!" When she looks at you, immediately tell her how clever she is and give her the food.

The way into your cat's heart is through her tummy! Always reward your cat for coming to you when you call with food, games, love, and affection.

Allow your cat to come to you, rather than trying to reach out to her. It's good cat manners!

Progress slowly

Over the next few days, continue to call your cat before you get her food out. Do this even when she is not in sight. This way she will be responding to the sound of your voice rather than the sound of the food bowl. If she doesn't come right away, wait and try again later. If she doesn't respond, don't be tempted to chase her—simply don't give her the food until she comes to you.

To make sure your cat will come when called no matter what the time or place, call her often and always reward her with different types of treats, her dinner, games, and toys. She'll always want to come running to you if there's something good waiting!

CAT FACT

The hearing of the average cat is at least 5 times better than that of a human and they can see up to 40 yards away, so if your cat doesn't come when you call, she's probably fast asleep or ignoring you!

TRAINING RULES:

- Cats need rewards for good behavior—just like us! Food, games, and attention all make good rewards.
- Never be cross if your cat takes a while to come when you call. It is better late than never!
- Never call your cat to you if you are then going to do something that she finds unpleasant, such as being treated for fleas, having her nails clipped, or being taken to the vet.
- Never try to grab your cat after you've called her to you. This will teach her to keep out of reach next time!
- If your cat is not in the mood for training, wait for a while until she seems more keen to interact or appears to be more interested in food.

Amazing tricks:
Sit on command and "be a bear"

Once you have mastered the basics, you can move on to the next level—coaxing your kitten or cat into different positions.

Sit on command

It's quite easy to train your cat to sit on command, just like a dog would. However, bear in mind that you cannot force a cat to sit. Instead, you must motivate her by offering a lure and then rewarding the correct behavior. After that, practice makes perfect!

1 Hold a treat between your fingers and thumb. Allow your cat to sniff the treat, but don't let her eat it.

2 Hold the treat slightly above her head so that her nose tips upward, toward the ceiling. As she lifts her head, her bottom will go down and she will sit naturally. As soon as this happens, say "good," then give her the treat.

3 Repeat this at least six times. If your cat's front paws come off the ground, your hand is a little too high. In this case, lower your hand slightly and hold on to the treat until she is sitting.

4 As soon as you think your cat has gotten the knack of following your hand, start to say the word "sit" just before you lure her. Say "good" and give her a treat every time she gets it right. Practice some more!

A star pupil! This little kitten is sitting patiently, waiting for her reward.

5 Now put the food treats in a bowl and place them out of the way. Ask your kitty to sit. Be patient. If your cat loses interest or walks away, rattle the treat bowl to let her know that good things are waiting for her. If she sits, act really pleased! Say "good" and give her a small handful of treats as a mega reward!

6 Practice asking your cat to sit in lots of different situations until she is sitting reliably to get her praise and rewards.

Amaze your friends and family! Cats can learn some impressive tricks.

"Be a bear"

Cats look adorable when they sit on their rear ends with their front legs raised. All you need to teach this trick is a handful of treats.

1 Lure your cat into a sitting position by following the guidelines above.

2 Now lift your hand up a bit so that your cat's front feet come off the ground slightly. Say "good" and give her a treat.

3 Repeat this until your cat lifts her feet a little higher off the ground. If she tries to grab the treat, ignore her and wait until she sits again.

4 Practice until your cat will balance on her bottom and bring her front feet off the ground as if she's begging. Cute!

TOP TIP
Never punish your cat if she doesn't do what you tell her. Simply stop training and wait until she is more attentive. Training should be fun!

Amazing tricks: Retrieve

Cats are often good at carrying things in their mouths, as this is natural behavior. However, not many people think of teaching their cat to retrieve items for them.

Most cats will happily chase after a moving toy, but they need gentle encouragement to bring it back again.

Teach your cat to retrieve

This can be a great game and can also provide your cat with some exercise as she dashes to get the toy and bring it back to you.

1 Choose a toy that your cat likes to play with. A small toy ball, a soft cat toy, and even a piece of foil screwed up into a tight ball are all appropriate.

2 Encourage your cat to be interested in the toy by playing with it yourself. Keep your voice low and your movements gentle, so that you do not frighten her. Wiggle the toy and make it appear and disappear so it looks like prey hiding behind the furniture. Most cats find a ball rolling past them almost irresistible!

3 Allow your cat to chase after the toy and pick it up. As soon as she does, encourage her to come towards you by moving away from her and calling her to you.

4 When your cat has come to you, praise her. Don't try to take the toy from her mouth as this may cause her to run off. Instead, allow her to drop it in exchange for a delicious treat or another toy.

5 Practice playing with your cat like this every day.

CAT FACT

Oriental breeds, such as Siamese cats, are natural retrievers and often pick this game up very quickly. Other cats may need time and patience to understand it.

Fixated: This
cat has spotted
her prey.

CAT FACT

Some cats discover that it's fun to retrieve things from other people's houses! There have been lots of cases of cats "stealing" items from other people's homes, or even from shops, and then bringing them home to their owners. Their "loot" can even include large items that they might struggle to get through the cat flap, such as whole packets of frozen ground beef! This strange behavior is thought to be an extension of natural maternal behavior, in which mother cats bring food home to their kittens.

Stay in control of the game

If your cat seems keen to chase a toy, but does not want to bring it back, you can encourage her by having another toy identical to the first one. As soon as she has chased one toy, start playing with the other by yourself. Guess which one she will want! Wait until she has come to you with the first toy before you throw the second toy for her to chase—that way you will always be in possession of one toy!

Training your cat to
retrieve uses her natural
hunting instincts.

Walking on a harness and leash

Teaching your cat to walk on a harness and long leash can be useful if you live in an area where it is not safe to let your cat out of doors. They can have the exercise and mental stimulation a walk provides, but without the risks of being hurt or getting lost.

Cats need to be taught to tolerate the feeling of the harness and leash, because it can give them greater freedom.

Getting started

Teaching a cat to walk on a leash takes much more time and patience than training a dog to, simply because cats do not like to be restrained in any way. Harness training tends to be easier if you start when your kitten is very young.

1 Choose a harness to fit your cat's shape and size, and make sure it is soft and comfortable. The straps should be adjustable, so that you can expand it as your kitten grows.

2 Fit the harness onto your kitten, giving her some treats to eat at the same time so that she is distracted. If she seems frightened or struggles, ask an adult to help you.

3 Make sure your kitten is calm and happy wearing the harness before you attach the leash. Put the harness on her when you feed her, play with her, and stroke her. She will soon start to associate wearing the harness with good things!

4 After several days of practicing this, you can attach a length of very lightweight cord to the harness and let it trail loose. This allows your kitten to get used to the feel of having something attached to the harness before you begin to hold the end.

5 Once your kitten seems happy with the cord, you can pick up the end of it. If she starts to move away, either drop the cord or follow her. Never jerk or pull on the cord, as this may frighten her.

Accustom your cat to wearing the harness by pairing it with good things, such as dinner.

6 Practice walking around the house with your kitten on the harness and leash for several days. When you want to change direction, call her by name and drop a treat on the ground beside you. She will learn to walk with you, not choose her own route!

TOP TIP
When training your kitten to walk on the harness and leash, never allow her to play with the end of the cord. If she gets into this habit, walking outdoors will be almost impossible!

7 Only when your kitten is totally relaxed about wearing the harness and leash can you go outside. She will probably want to stop and look at all the sights and sniff all the lovely smells, so take your time and allow her to enjoy herself. Take her out for walks daily, so that she becomes used to the area and gains confidence outdoors.

Camping capers

Teaching your cat to walk on a harness and leash means that she can come on holiday with you! Some owners take their cats with them in their RVs, so that they can enjoy a vacation together in the great outdoors!

The one that got away! Once confident on the harness and leash, your cat may even be able to accompany you on vacation!

Fun and Games

Fun and games should not be occasional extras for your cat—they should be part of her everyday life. This is especially true if your cat is kept indoors. When they are outdoors, cats spend a lot of time hunting or preparing to hunt. If your cat is kept indoors, offering play and games can be a way of allowing her to use her natural instincts without treating you like a giant mouse!

Although it's important that both you and your cat enjoy the games you play, first and foremost you should play the games your cat would choose. Quite clearly, these will not include football or chess, but that's not to say that physical games and mind-stretching puzzles aren't on her list. Try to think about how your cat experiences the world and play games that fit in with what she enjoys doing—stalking, chasing, and hunting are all feline favorites! Perhaps the worst fate for any cat is to be stuck indoors and bored. Without mental and physical stimulation cats can become depressed, lethargic, overweight, and even aggressive.

Make sure you give your cat plenty to do, both while you are there to keep her company and when she's left alone. Your cat's life should be filled with fun and games— you will love it, too!

Playing games with your cat should be a part of your everyday fun with her.

Chase games: Playing safe

Cats are incredible hunting machines! Although they look cute cuddled up on their beds indoors, once they are outside, they can switch on their predator instincts to find, stalk, chase, and catch prey.

Their eyes are perfectly designed to catch the smallest movement, using their peripheral vision (side vision—the ability to see objects and movement outside of the direct line of sight). Their sense of smell can detect crushed vegetation where other animals have trodden as well as the scent of the animals themselves, and their hearing can pick up the tiniest squeak from many feet away.

All these incredible abilities need to be channeled and exercised for your cat to be content, but how can you do this without sacrificing real mice or your fingers? The answer is that we must understand what it is exactly that triggers our cats to hunt and find ways of imitating a hunt in a safe and enjoyable way.

Keep your fingers well out of reach when playing with your kitten or cat.

SIMPLE STRING

Drag a long piece of string slowly around the furniture, just out of your cat's reach. The movement of it disappearing out of sight will have her using the sofa as cover while she plays commando trying to ambush the imaginary mouse!

Fishing rod toy

Some of the best toys for your cat are ones that you can make for free! They may be simple, but your cat will love playing with them.

1 You will need a length of bamboo cane, about 12 inches long. A stick of another light, smooth type of wood will also be fine. If the length needs cutting, ask an adult to help you.

2 Wrap the ends of the stick with plastic tape so they are safe to handle.

3 Tie a long piece of string on to one end of the stick and secure the string with some more tape.

4 Tie a feather or pieces of ribbon to the free end of the string. You will find that they "fly" beautifully and are perfect for your cat to stalk, pounce on, and chase.

Hand in glove

If you have an old glove, you can transform it into the perfect kitty toy by asking an adult to help you sew some long pieces of thick cotton to the fingers. Leave these dangling down and tie lightweight objects, such as feathers or rolled balls of foil, to the ends. You can then put the glove on your hand and make the strings dance by wiggling your fingers. Cat heaven!

Mouse movement

A cat's desire to hunt is not caused by hunger. Cats have been known to break away from eating a plate of delicious food to spring on prey, then go back immediately and resume their dinner! Instead, it appears that cats are triggered into chasing automatically when they detect a certain kind of movement. This movement is quick, and away from the cat rather than towards it—the kind of movement that a mouse might make when running away. You can use this knowledge when playing with your cat by making your cat toy look and act like prey, such as a mouse's tail. You will notice immediately that if you wiggle the toy away from your cat, and even make it "hide" behind furniture, she will be far keener to chase it than if it simply stays still.

Cats love to stalk, chase, and pounce. Giving them a safe outlet for "hunting" is essential, particularly if your cat lives indoors.

Hunt the "mouse"! Searching games

Searching and stalking together make up a large part of the hunting process. Cats use their eyes, ears, and noses to find prey, so try to involve all their senses when playing searching games.

TOP TIP

The first rule when playing with your cat is to understand that she has teeth and claws, and that they are sharp! Your cat may not mean to hurt you in play, but if she views your hands or clothes as playthings, she might scratch or bite you by accident. Because of this, it's important to always use a toy when playing with your cat. The longer the toy, the better for you both.

UNDER THE CUP

This game makes your cat look very clever, as it uses her ability to sniff out food.

You will need:
- Some delicious treats, such as tiny pieces of cooked chicken
- A lightweight plastic cup

Rules of the game:
- Place a delicious treat under the upturned cup.
- Ask your cat to find the treat. You can help her a little to begin with by lifting the cup to show her the treat underneath.

Once your cat is confident with this game, try placing the tidbit inside a cardboard tube and see whether she can find it and hook it out with a paw.

Magic tricks for cats—now you see it, now you don't!

It's in the bag

For some reason cats just love playing with bags they can climb into—the scrunchier the better!

1 Choose a large paper bag (never a plastic one).

2 Scrunch up the neck of the bag a little and blow into it to inflate it slightly.

3 Place a few dry treats inside the bag and watch your kitten figure out how to get them by pouncing on the bag and rummaging inside it.

BALL IN THE BOX

For this game you will need a shallow cardboard box. Ask an adult to help if you need to cut a deeper box down so that your cat can comfortably reach inside it with her paw.

Put a small, lightweight ball (such as a Ping-Pong ball) into the box and roll it around so that your cat can chase it about with her paw. To make this toy even more exciting, you can place the box on an uneven surface (a pencil placed on the floor under the box will do the job). This makes the box tip slightly. When she bats the ball, it will roll in a completely new direction.

CAT FACT

Catnip is the popular name for a plant called nepeta, which is found growing in gardens across the world. This plant has a chemical within its stem and leaves called nepetalactone. This chemical can have the most amazing effect on some cats, causing them to rub on the plant and roll in it as though they are in an enjoyable trance!

This game allows your cat to chase an imaginary mouse.

Cat agility!

Agility isn't only for dogs! Cats love using their natural abilities to jump, run, spring, and climb, and a home agility course or "gym" is the perfect way for them to let off steam.

Tunnel of fun

You can buy special pet play tunnels—your cat may appreciate one for her birthday. However, a homemade one will do just as well! You will need a large cardboard box.

Even kittens can learn to navigate their way through play tunnels.

1 Turn the box upside down and mark a tunnel opening using felt pen on each end of the box. Ask an adult to help you cut out the tunnel entrance and exit if it is difficult. Make these openings at least twice as big as your cat!

2 Place the box on the floor and encourage your cat to walk into the tunnel by pulling a piece of string through from one end or by hiding a tidbit in the middle so that she goes in to explore.

3 Once your cat is confident about entering the tunnel you need to be able to get her out again, so call her to you and reward her when she comes running!

Cats are naturally agile and can enjoy negotiating obstacles indoors if they are motivated.

JUMP FOR JOY

Cats are excellent at jumping, but they need to be given a reason for doing it! Never try to force your cat to jump. Instead, lure her with a treat or encourage her to follow a favorite toy. This should be fun for both of you.

Prop a lightweight cane on the top of two upturned flowerpots of the same height, two plastic cones bought from a toy shop, or any objects that will support the stick at either end to make a hurdle. Make sure you set the height of the hurdle so that your cat will leap over it rather than be tempted to squeeze underneath.

Everyday obstacles

Teach your cat to jump onto a footstool and then leap from there to a non-slip chair nearby, and so on. You can begin by teaching her to expect a treat on the footstool.

1 Place a treat on top of the footstool. Encourage your cat to jump up there by patting the top and talking to her. If she seems reluctant, you can gently lift her up and place her on the stool to eat the treat, but she must do it on her own next time!

2 Repeat this at least six times, making sure she is rewarded each time.

3 As soon as your cat is anticipating food on the footstool, encourage her up and then give her the treat when she is on top. Now she is ready to move on to the next stage.

4 Position a chair very close to the footstool and place a treat on the seat. Hopefully, your cat will step across from the stool. However, if she gets down from the stool, you will need to remove the treat quickly and start over again.

5 Once your cat is really confident about getting up onto the stool and stepping from there across to the chair, you can start to move the two platforms a little farther apart. Move them just an inch or two each time until she is jumping between the two.

The whole course!

Now you can put your whole agility course together. Lead your cat through the tunnel, onto the footstool, onto the chair, down again, and over the hurdle to finish! Want to do more? Put the equipment in a circle and then lead your cat through the obstacles in different sequences!

One giant leap! Encourage your cat to jump onto a safe surface as a part of your agility course.

Cat intelligence tests

How bright is your cat? Can she outwit the average dog? Of course your cat is intelligent! After all, she can figure out when you are going to feed her, when you come home from school, and how to get you to play with her.

Testing intelligence in animals is difficult, because they are not designed to take math exams or write essays! Instead, we can test whether or not an animal can solve puzzles or remember how to get something that they want. You can set up your own intelligence test for your cat, just for fun!

Just how bright is your cat? Take our test and see if she's a genius.

JUST LIKE THAT!

For the first puzzle, you will need:
- 🐾 Three old plastic cups
- 🐾 Treats

Place the three cups upside down and place some treats under only one of them. Encourage your cat to hunt for the treats and then get to them by pushing over the correct cup.

Does she:
a) Go straight to the correct cup and knock it over to get to the treats? Score 5.

b) Knock over one of the other cups before finding and knocking over the right one? Score 3.

c) Knock over both the wrong cups before finding the right one? Score 1.

OPEN THE DOOR

For the second puzzle, you will need:
- 🐾 A cat carrier with a door
- 🐾 Treats

Place the carrier on the ground so that it is at your cat's level. While your cat is watching, place some yummy treats inside the carrier and then push the door closed with your cat on the *outside*.

Watch your cat carefully. Does she:
a) Approach the door and try to open it by using her paw or nose? Score 5.

b) Approach the carrier and walk around and around it, looking in at the treats? Score 3.

c) Walk away? Score 1.

MAZE TEST

For the third puzzle, you will need:

🐾 A stopwatch or second counter on a clock or watch

🐾 Four cardboard boxes

🐾 Treats

Preparation: Arrange the cardboard boxes in a square, with a single path into the middle of the square, formed by a gap between two of the boxes.

Place a few treats in the center of the square. Hold your cat so that she can see the gap, then release her so that she walks through the gap to get to the treats.

Now place more treats in the center, but this time, take your cat around to the other side of the boxes so she can't see the way in. Time how long it takes her to walk back around to the gap, go through, and find the treats.

a) Less than 20 seconds. Score 5.

b) 20–60 seconds. Score 3.

c) More than one minute. Score 1.

Setting up a maze for your cat is easy and fun—see just how complex you can make it for an advanced version!

See how quickly your cat can work out how to open the door to get inside.

Your cat's scores

10–15 points: Wow! Your cat is a genius!

5–10 points: Well done. Your cat works hard to find the right answers.

0–5 points: Could try harder. Of course, it's also possible that your cat is very clever and simply didn't want to do any hard work!

Questions you've always wanted to ask!

Can my cat watch television?

Some cats do appear to watch television, but of course they cannot tell us what they see! Cats do not see colors as we do—they see reds as shades of gray, for example. The picture on a TV screen is comprised of red, blue, and green dots. We see the colors on TV as being a mixture of these, but cats will only see the colors produced by combining blue, green, and gray. This might mean that they find it difficult to see some images at all. Despite this, videos and DVDs for cats have been produced, based on what they might like to watch! Certainly, some cats seem to enjoy watching pictures of fish swimming and butterflies and moths flying—some will even bat the front of the TV screen as if they are trying to catch them!

If your kitten bounces around in the evenings, she may simply be using up some excess energy.

Why does my cat have a "mad half hour"?

Many kittens seem to have a mad half hour in the evenings after dinner. They may suddenly leap up and race around the room using the furniture as an obstacle course, and their owners, too, if they happen to be in the way!

No one really knows what causes this odd behavior in kittens, but it's likely that it releases pent-up energy at the end of the day. It's important that your kitten learns she can't pounce on you or bite you as part of her fun. Either distract her with an exciting toy, play a game to tire her out, or get up and walk out of the room if she persists in trying to treat you like a giant mouse!

Some cats watch TV and even seem to have favorite programs!

Stalking birds is natural cat behavior. Your cat might even bring one home as a gift!

Why do cats bring home mice and birds?

It's a natural instinct for cats to want to chase mice, birds, sometimes insects, and even larger prey, such as squirrels and rabbits. Actually, this ability to hunt rodents is one of the reasons why people encouraged cats to live around them to begin with. However, rather than just catching, killing, and eating their prey outdoors, cats often bring them home—and make a special effort to show us what they have brought.

If you discover that your cat has brought you a little "gift," don't be cross with her. You cat is simply following her need to treat you as a part of her family. She might be bringing home food for you as though you were one of her kittens that had not yet learned how to hunt for itself. This explains why she might sometimes bring back prey that is still alive, so that she can teach you how to stalk, pounce on, and kill the prey!

Sphynx cats are hairless, which makes them less likely to cause allergies for some people.

What causes cat allergies?

Some people are allergic to cats. Allergies can be triggered by a cat's hair, dead skin that flakes off its body, or, more commonly, the cat's saliva, which is on the coat after they lick themselves. Some breeds of cats—such as hairless varieties—may not cause this reaction in everyone with an allergy, but this can only be established on an individual basis, as all cats lick themselves, whether or not they have hair.

Questions you've always wanted to ask!

Why do cats dig in flower beds?

Cats are very clean animals, which means that they nearly always like to cover up the area after they have been to the toilet. This is why they scratch around in their litter box or in soil outside before and after they have been to the toilet. First, they scrape a small hole. After they have gone, they cover it up with fresh litter or soil. Flower beds are perfect for this. The soil is light and crumbly, making it easy to dig in and comfortable to crouch on! Gardeners may not be too pleased about these toilet arrangements!

On occasion your cat may leave her toilet area uncovered, deliberately leaving her feces visible. This acts as a scent signal to other cats and animals. The behavior is called "middening."

Does my cat dream, just like me?

It's impossible to know for sure if cats dream just like we do. However, if you've ever watched your cat when she's fast asleep, you will know that sometimes her whiskers, her paws, or even her tail might twitch as if she's dreaming. Cats can even be heard growling or purring while asleep occasionally, so perhaps they go out hunting or chasing in their dreams!

Cats can sleep for many hours of the day. In fact, the average cat naps for 13–18 hours every day to save energy and pass the time. Cats in the wild are diurnal, which means they are most active in the early morning and evenings, when they do most of their hunting. Domestic cats adjust to our routines. After all, it's more fun to be awake when we are, and to sleep at night.

Cats just love flower beds to use as toilet areas, as the soil is light and loose.

Not many cats like water, but the
Turkish Van is the exception—they
just love swimming!

Can cats swim?

Cats can swim, but most of them hate it
because they simply don't like getting wet!
There is a notable exception, however. The
Turkish Van cat is famous for its love of
water. Some cats of this breed even enjoy
dripping taps. They will drink from them or
flick the water up with their paws. Others
have a fascination for swimming—in the bath,
if possible, or even in the sea! If you have a
cat of this breed you'll soon discover that it's
always best to keep the toilet lid down!

Why does my cat lick herself?

Cats lick themselves to clean their coats.
Licking also serves to help regulate their
body temperature. By smoothing down
their coats, they trap in warm air, which
keeps them warm. In hotter weather, their
saliva evaporates off the hair, helping keep
them cool.

As you know, a cat's tongue is very rough.
This texture is created by hundreds of tiny,
backwards-facing hooks, which together
act as a mini brush. They help remove
parasites and loose hairs, which are then
swallowed—these are sometimes brought
back up as furballs later on.

Cats also lick themselves for
reassurance—this is why your cat might
lick herself more after you've been stroking
her or playing with her, or if something
worries her. Cats that get along well
together also groom and lick each other.
This helps spread their communal scent
and increase their bonding.

Cats lick themselves to
keep clean, to maintain
their coats, and to
reassure themselves.

Questions you've always wanted to ask!

Why does my cat have such big teeth?

Cats are predators. They are designed to stalk, chase, and pounce, and they are formidable killers of small rodents, birds, and other creatures. Their long, fanglike front teeth—their "canine" teeth—are specially designed weapons used to catch and kill their prey.

Why does my cat sometimes run away from me?

Some cats are more nervous than others. This seems to be a genetic factor—a cat's personality and temperament seem to be largely inherited from her father. However, all cats are prone to being startled by sudden movements, loud noises, and unexpected events. In these cases, they tend to run first and ask questions later! This is usually a good survival strategy as it helps to keep cats out of trouble. Occasionally, a cat may not recognize someone she knows and may run a short distance before recovering herself and returning to be friendly.

Cats also learn very quickly to avoid things that they don't like. If you spray your cat with flea treatment one day, don't be surprised if she runs off when she sees you carrying the spray can again the following day!

Why does my cat dribble and knead me with her paws?

Outside your cat may be a wild predator, but indoors she's as dependent on you as if she were a baby! Cats revert to many kittenish behaviors when they are indoors with people who they know and trust. This might include kneading their paws against you if they are cuddling and dribbling at the same time. This behavior comes from the time when your cat kneaded her mother to stimulate her milk flow. This action made her salivate in anticipation. Now she's blissfully and contentedly doing the same thing to you!

Why does my cat seem to want to go to people who don't like cats?

Cat language is different from human language. One of the biggest differences is that in cat language, closing your eyes and turning your face and body away looks like an invitation to be friendly. It would mean completely the opposite to a person! People who don't like cats tend to ignore them and turn away from them, but the cat sees this as a polite way of asking her to approach!

Glossary

Adolescence The period from around 5–18 months of age, in which your cat is the equivalent of a human teenager.

Agility course An obstacle course, including jumps, tunnels, or raised walkways.

Body language A cat's use of body postures and facial expressions to communicate.

Carrier Used to safely contain and transport your cat, made of strong cardboard, plastic, or wire.

Catnip An herb called nepeta. Some cats respond to catnip as if they are in heaven—rolling in it and tasting it! Others ignore it completely. This seems to be an inherited response.

Clan odor The scent that makes your whole family smell the same to your cat.

Command The word you say when you want your cat to move into a particular position, such as "sit," or perform a trick, such as "be a bear."

Ear mites Mites that live in a cat's ear canal. They cause irritation and the buildup of dark brown wax. Vet treatment is required for ear mites.

Feline A word that is used to describe all things cat, which comes from the Latin term *feli*.

Feral cats Cats that have not been socialized with people and live in a wild state.

Grooming Brushing, combing, nail clipping, and teeth brushing for your cat.

Growl A low, rumbling sound cats sometimes make in their throats—usually a warning signal.

Hairball/furball A mass of hair swallowed during grooming that lodges in a cat's stomach and may be vomited up.

Harness A piece of equipment that fits around a cat's body and chest, which can be attached to a leash.

Kitten A young cat, under the age of six months old.

Litter Material placed in a litter box to absorb liquids and reduce odor. Litter can be wood chips, clay pellets, or sand.

Littermates A cat's brothers and sisters.

Lure To use a tidbit to encourage your cat into the position you want.

Predator An animal that hunts and eats other animals in order to survive.

Prey An animal that is caught and eaten by another animal as food.

Purring Vibrations in a cat's throat that make a distinctive sound—usually to show she is happy and content.

Queen An un-neutered, adult female cat.

Reward Anything your cat likes in return for doing something good; usually a treat or a game with a toy.

Socialization Introducing your cat to lots of people, so that she gets used to communicating with them.

Spraying Characteristic urine marking behavior, in which cats squirt urine on vertical surfaces.

Tom An un-neutered adult male cat.

Treat A small piece of food that your cat likes, such as cooked chicken.

Vet An animal doctor.

Vocalization Any sound that your cat makes with her mouth and throat.

Wet/dry food Wet cat food comes in cans. Dry cat food is in pellets and often comes in a box or sack.

Web sites

www.aspca.org/animaland
American Society for the Prevention of Cruelty to Animals (ASPCA) Animaland—for kids who love animals.

http://www.cfainc.org
The Cat Fanciers Association site, which gives information on breeds and showing as well as quizzes, stories, and puzzles.

www.bestfriends.org/theanimals/petcare/cats
Cat-specific advice from the Best Friends Animal Society in the United States.

Talk to your friends who also have cats and exchange ideas.

www.cats.org.uk/catsforkids
Cats Protection is a United Kingdom-based site, with lots of fun information and care tips, as well as cute wallpapers to download and ideas for cat toys to make.

www.kittynames.com
Find out what the name of your cat means, or choose a name for your new cat.

www.peteducation.com
A useful site for parents with solutions to common problems.

Organizations

United States and Canada

Best Friends Animal Society
5001 Angel Canyon Road
Kanab, UT 84741-5001
Tel: (435) 644-2001
www.bestfriends.org

Cat Fanciers Association
1805 Atlantic Avenue
P.O. Box 1005
Manasquan, NJ 08736-0805
Ph: (732) 528-7391
Email: cfa@cfa.org
www.cfainc.org

Canadian Cat Association
289 Rutherford Road, S # 18
Brampton ON, L6W 3R9
Ph: (905) 459-1481
Email: office@cca-afc.com
www.cca-afc.com

United Kingdom

The Pet Advisory Committee
1 Bedford Avenue
London WC1B 3AU
Tel: (020) 7255-5489
www.petadvisory.org.uk

Cat Fancy U.K.
5 King's Castle Business Park
The Drove, Bridgewater
Somerset, TA6 4AG
Ph: (01278) 427-575
www.gccfcats.org

Australia and New Zealand

Australian Cat Federation (Inc.)
Secretary
P.O. Box 331
Port Adelaide BC SA 5015
Ph: (08) 8449-5880
Email:acfinc@chariot.net.au

New Zealand Cat Fancy
Private Bag 6103
Napier
Ph: (06) 839-7811
Email: secretary@nzcf.com
www.nzcatfancy.gen.nz

**Cats are loved in
millions of households
all around the world!**

Index

Acknowledgments

Photography

Photographs are by John Daniels, with the
following exceptions:
Quarto, Inc. London 2, 16bl, 21tr, 24, 26t, 37tl,
38tr, 46tr, 51br, 58tr, 64bl, 71tl, 85bl, 90ml;
Warren Photographic 11br top & middle, 13tl,
33tl, 35tr, 87tl; David King 29br; Kim Taylor/
Bruce Coleman 11br bottom; Hans Reinhard/
Bruce Coleman16tr; © Pat Doyle/Corbis 40tr.